Introduction

The Writing Process

Writing is a thinking process. Someone once said, "It is a continuous struggle to discover what you have to say and how to say it." When writers write, they engage in that struggle as they move through a series of steps enroute to publication:

- **Prewriting**
  They gather impressions, thoughts, facts, and questions as they search for what they want to say.

- **First Draft Writing**
  They begin composing. They write down their thoughts.

- **Responding, Revising, Editing**
  They look at their first draft, rereading with an eye for sense and readability. They rewrite and revise to refine the text. Corrections in grammar and mechanics are made. The writing is fine-tuned.

- **Publishing**
  The writing is produced in "finished" form.

Using This Book

Writing Fabulous Sentences & Paragraphs begins with a brief review of the parts of a sentence, types of sentences, and ending punctuation (pages 7-13). Depending on the level of your group, you may wish to skip this section.

Succeeding lessons and activities progress from the writing of sentences to the writing of paragraphs. The materials are meant to model and practice the basic components of writing; to aid students in clarifying thinking; and to sharpen writing skills.

Always move beyond this practice to "real-life" paragraph writing experiences. The best writing experiences grow out of student interests and needs. Choose the lessons that are appropriate for your students and your curriculum.

Getting Started

Keeping Writing Folders

Writing folders are a valuable aid in a successful writing program. They organize writing samples, act as an idea bank, document progress, and serve as a resource for parent education.

Writing folders can be as simple as a folder with a contents sheet (such as the one provided on page 3) stapled inside.

Use the writing folders to:
- Store Student Writing
    Students should date and file their writing samples. When a sample is added, it is recorded on the contents sheet.
- Generate Ideas
    Students can review samples to choose a piece that they would like to develop further. Students can reread or refer to previous writing as they edit and revise current writing.
- Document Student Progress
    It is valuable to compare pieces written at the beginning of the year with pieces written at the end of the year. Look at the paper with specific objectives in mind and document growth in achieving those objectives.

Individual Writing Conferences

As your students practice sentence and paragraph writing, meet with them to discuss their individual progress and possible areas for growth.

1. Choose a writing sample from the writing folder.
2. Discuss and evaluate the sample for specific skills.
3. Record strengths and areas that need improvement.
4. Develop a goal for future writing.

Evaluation Forms

1. Paragraph Conference Form (page 4).
   Use this as a part of individual writing conferences.

2. Analyze Your Sentence (page 5).
   This list of questions allows students to focus on the key features of a single sentence and then apply this knowledge to their own sentence writing.

3. Paragraph Skills Checklist (page 6).
   Use this checklist to identify specific skills that need to be emphasized in your writing instruction.

Writing Folder Contents

Date	Name of Piece	Comments

Writing Fabulous Sentences & Paragraphs EMC 575

Paragraph Conference Form

Name _____

Date _____

Title _____

What is the purpose of the paragraph? _____

_____

What is the topic of the paragraph? _____

_____

What is the topic sentence of the paragraph? _____

_____

What are the supporting details? _____

_____

How is the paragraph organized? _____

_____

Strengths of the Paragraph   Things to Work On

_____   _____

_____   _____

Goal: _____

_____

Analyze Your Sentence

What is the purpose of your sentence?

____to tell something

____to ask something

____to give directions

What punctuation ends your sentence? Why?

What is the subject of your sentence?

What is the predicate of your sentence?

What words tell the reader about the subject?

What words tell the reader about the predicate?

Paragraph Skills Checklist

Identifies topic of paragraph												
Chooses a good topic sentence												
Identifies supporting details												
Identifies extraneous details												
Writes a good topic sentence given the topic and the supporting details												
Writes supporting details given the topic sentence												
Indents the first line of a paragraph												
Uses correct capitalization and punctuation												
Uses a web to plan and write a paragraph												
Writes descriptive paragraphs • guided												
• independently												
Writes narrative paragraphs • guided												
• independently												
Writes paragraphs to compare and contrast • guided												
• independently												
Writes persuasive paragraphs • guided												
• independently												
Writes paragraphs to define • guided												
• independently												
Uses a web to plan and write a multiple-paragraph piece												
Uses an outline to plan and write several paragraphs												
Uses paragraphing consistently in all writing												

Writing Fabulous Sentences & Paragraphs EMC 575

What Is a Sentence?

Reviewing the Concept of Sentence

- Not all groups of words are sentences. Sentences must have two things:

    1. A Subject
    A subject is the noun, noun phrase, or pronoun in a sentence that does the action or is described by the predicate.

    2. A Predicate
    The predicate tells about the subject. Grammarians say that it modifies the subject. It must include a verb, and may include objects, or phrases governed by verb.

- When you teach about sentences, use real examples at first to help students connect this information with their own experiences:

Example 1	• Have a student stand up and walk to the door.
	• Ask your class to tell what happened.
	
	        Sally went to the door.
	
	• This is a sentence. It tells **who**, *Sally*, and it tells **what** Sally did, *went to the door*.
	
	• Either part, by itself, is not a sentence.
	     Sally is not a sentence.
	     went to the door is not a sentence.

Example 2	• Ask your class to describe your classroom.
	
	    Room 12 is a crowded classroom.
	
	• This is a sentence. The subject is *Room 12*.
	  The predicate tells about the subject, *is a crowded classroom*.

Identifying Sentences

After your students understand the terms subject and predicate, have them practice identifying sentences and their components. Use work pages like those on pages 8 and 9 for guided practice.

Then have students identify the components of sentences in their own writing. Begin by copying student sentences on a transparency and identifying the subject and predicate as a group. Move from there to having students mark the subjects and predicates on a paper of their own. Pairs can discuss each other's responses.

Name _____

Can You Find the Sentences?

Find the groups of words that are sentences.
Label their parts:

1. Circle the subject of the sentence.

2. Draw a line under the predicate of the sentence.

Write "sentence" on the line following each complete sentence.

Tom and Julie played ball   _____

Climbed the mountain and camped   _____

The class went to the library   _____

Marilyn ate her lunch   _____

Susan, Bill, and Jack   _____

The flag waved in the wind   _____

The girl stumbled forward   _____

Always busy working in the kitchen, the cooks   _____

The soccer ball flew into the goal   _____

The computer responded to his command   _____

On the back of this page, make each **non-sentence** into a **sentence**.

Name _____

Subjects and Predicates

1. Write **S** in front of the subjects.
2. Write **P** in front of the predicates.
3. Make three sentences by combining subjects and predicates.

_____ the workers

_____ learning

_____ ambled home

_____ Sylvia and Arby

_____ chased me home

_____ can be fun

_____ hurricanes

_____ the puppies

_____ were busy

_____ frighten me

Sentences:

1. _____

   _____

2. _____

   _____

3. _____

   _____

Note: Make a transparency or chart of this page to discuss types of sentences.
Pages 11-13 can be reproduced to practice punctuation skills.

Kinds of Sentences

Declarative Sentence

- tells something
- ends with a period

That tree with brightly colored leaves is a sugar maple.

Interrogative Sentence (Question)

- asks something
- ends with a question mark

Is maple syrup made from the sap of the sugar maple?

Exclamatory Sentence

- shouts something
- ends with an exclamation mark

Wow, those pancakes with maple syrup are delicious!

Name _____

Different Kinds of Sentences

Read this conversation between a mother and a son. Then add the correct end punctuation to each sentence. Label each sentence:

I for an interrogative sentence
D for a declarative sentence
E for an exclamatory sentence

_____ **Mom**: Don't touch the iron

_____ **Son**: Why not

_____ **Mom**: I've just been pressing your father's pants

_____ **Mom**: You'll burn yourself if you touch it

_____ **Son**: What good does it do to iron Dad's pants

_____ **Son**: He just sits down and wrinkles them again

_____ **Mom**: It does seem never ending, but it's nice to start out looking neat

_____ **Mom**: Don't you like looking neat

_____ **Son**: I think part of looking neat is being wrinkled

_____ **Son**: Boy, am I glad that I don't have to be ironed to im**press** my friends

With a partner, read the sentences aloud with expression that shows the punctuation you chose.

Name _____

Writing
Sentences

Write at least five sentences of your own.
Circle the subject of your sentences.
Underline the predicate.
Be sure to use the correct end punctuation.

_____

_____

_____

_____

_____

_____

_____

_____

_____

_____

_____

_____

Make It Easy to Read

Punctuation helps the reader to understand what the writer is saying. Add end punctuation to the sentences in this piece. Is it easier to read with punctuation in place?

From the Journal of a Crayon

"Boy, is it crowded in here That Jungle Green is in my spot Will you please move I wish that they would make these boxes bigger "

"Stop complaining Soon one of us will be lost or broken and then there'll be plenty of room "

I listened and observed as the hushed conversation in my crayon-box home droned on It was a new sixty-four color box with a tight lid and bright yellow and green triangles covering its front Few crayon users realize that crayons not only speak but they also have feelings Just the other day, I witnessed the dismay of a canary yellow whose tip was nibbled off by a hungry artist, and the sorrow of a twenty-box that had lost its black Imagine life without a black Well, it is true that crayons do have the sensitive souls of artists and it is time for all humankind to recognize it How can we as crayons make our position known

I have taken it upon myself to represent the crayon world I will present a case for our humane treatment at the National Rights Conference to be held in Washington, D.C., on June 1 Soon all crayons will enjoy the notoriety of Harold's purple crayon It will be a red-letter day for all writers of color

Combining Sentences

As your students write sentences successfully, point out that often the information included in two sentences can be combined into one sentence. Combining ideas makes writing more interesting by eliminating short, choppy sentences.

Pages 15, 17, and 19 illustrate three ways that two ideas can be combined into a single sentence. Reproduce each page on a transparency or chart. Follow up the presentation of each sentence-combining technique by having small groups of students generate their own examples to share with the class. Individual practice is provided for by follow-up worksheets (pages 16, 18, 20, 21, and 22).

You may want to enlarge each chart on the photocopier and post it for student reference. Throughout the year, as students begin a writing assignment, remind them to use the charts for help in making their sentences varied and interesting.

Make combining sentences a skill you notice during writing conferences with individual students.

Combining Two Ideas in a Single Sentence

Chart
1

Turn one of the sentences into a phrase and place it at the beginning to tell about the subject of your sentence.

Two related ideas:

Tom went to the mall.

He looked for a new hat there.

One sentence:

When Tom went to the mall, he looked for a new hat.

Two related ideas:

Penny got out of bed.

She looked out her window to check the weather.

One sentence:

When Penny got out of bed, she looked out her window to check the weather.

Name _____

Combining Two Ideas in a Single Sentence

For each pair of sentences, write one sentence that includes the ideas from both sentences. Turn one of the sentences into a phrase and place it at the beginning to tell about the subject of your sentence.

1. The football team ran onto the field. They carried their helmets in their hands.

   _____

   _____

2. Pam found a book for her report. She used the library browser on the computer.

   _____

   _____

3. The clown ran around the elephant. The elephant squirted water on the clown.

   _____

   _____

4. I called Joe on the telephone. He sounded like he didn't feel well.

   _____

   _____

5. There was a snowstorm during the night. This morning the fenceposts poked their tops above the drifts.

   _____

   _____

6. Tom fell off the bike. He learned that racing bikes can be dangerous.

   _____

   _____

Combining Two Ideas in a Single Sentence

Chart 2

When one of the two sentences names the subject, include that information as a modifying phrase after the subject in the sentence. Use commas to identify the phrase.

Two related ideas:

Shadow is my cat.

She hates lightning and thunder.

One sentence:

Shadow, my cat, hates lightning and thunder.

Two related ideas:

Mr. Christian is my principal.

He always smiles when I pass him in the hall.

One sentence:

Mr. Christian, my principal, always smiles when I pass him in the hall.

Name _____

Combining Two Ideas in a Single Sentence

Combine each pair of ideas into a single sentence by including information in a **modifying phrase** after the subject in the sentence.

honey

my favorite treat

1. John is my little brother.

   He is a good shortstop.

   _____

2. Sandy is a frisky puppy.

   She likes to chase the cat.

   _____

3. Scott's goldfish was named Force of Freedom.

   It survived for five years.

   _____

4. Sandy, Carlos, and Willy are my friends.

   We like to play at the park.

   _____

5. Mr. Sutter is my coach.

   He taught me how to hit the ball hard.

   _____

6. Ashley lives next door to me.

   She feeds my puppies when I'm gone.

   _____

Combining Two Ideas in a Single Sentence

Chart 3

You can combine two sentences using the important words from each sentence and a connecting word such as **and, to, but, since, because,** ....

Two related sentences:

> Sarah and Sean went to a lake in Rocky Mountain National Park.
>
> They wanted to go hiking.

One sentence:

> Sarah and Sean went to a lake in Rocky Mountain National Park to go hiking.

Two related sentences:

> Sam learned to do a back flip.
>
> He learned to do a cartwheel, too.

One sentence:

> Sam learned to do a back flip and a cartwheel, too.

Two related sentences:

> We drove to the supermarket to get milk.
>
> When we got there the store was closed.

One sentence:

> We drove to the supermarket to get milk, but when we got there the store was closed.

Two related sentences:

> Ahmad is our new student body president.
>
> He got the most votes in the election.

One sentence:

> Ahmad is our new student body president because he got the most votes in the election.

Name _____

Combining Two Ideas
in a Single Sentence

Using the two sentences given, write one sentence using a connecting word such as **and, to, but, since,** or **because**.

1. Grandma made chocolate chip cookies for me. She made snickerdoodles for my brother Jim.

_____

_____

2. The horse nibbled the hay. He swished his tail to keep the flies away.

_____

_____

3. My umbrella broke when the wind blew. I got soaked.

_____

_____

4. Mowing the lawn is hard work. My mom always brings me lemonade when I finish.

_____

_____

5. The mail carrier brought a package. It's my father's birthday today.

_____

_____

6. My glasses steamed up when I went inside. It was freezing outside.

_____

_____

Name _____

Put Them Together

Practice combining two sentences into one.

1. Read the two sentences.
2. Write one new sentence that includes the information from both sentences.

---

1. Autumn is a season of the year. It is sometimes called Fall.

_____

_____

2. The leaves turn color. Squirrels begin to store seeds for the winter.

_____

_____

3. The air is crisp and cold. Spectators don coats and gloves.

_____

_____

4. The sun is sleeping when I get up. It goes to bed while I eat my dinner.

_____

_____

5. Autumn is a celebration of the harvest. Autumn is a warning to prepare for the cold days ahead.

_____

_____

Name _____

Combining Sentences

Write two short related sentences that you have found in your writing.

Combine the two sentences into one single sentence that contains all the same information.

1. _____

2. _____

Combined

_____

_____

Name _____

Combining Sentences

Write two short related sentences that you have found in your writing.

Combine the two sentences into one single sentence that contains all the same information.

1. _____

2. _____

Combined

_____

_____

Using Descriptive Details

Sentences are more interesting and informative if they include descriptive details. Consider which of the sentences in the following pairs gives a clearer, more dynamic picture.

The boys had ice cream for dessert.

For dessert, the boys had chocolate ice cream with swirls of peanut butter, chunks of dark chocolate, and bits of almonds.

The bike leaned against the tree.

The bike, a rusty three-speed that had seen better days, was leaning against the tree.

Writers see pictures in their own minds and work to find the words to create the same pictures in the minds of their readers.

The activities on pages 24- 31 will help your students to write sentences that create pictures.

This Is Me!

Encourage students to think about details by describing themselves. Have mirrors available. Use page 24 and 25 to help students look at themselves closely and then write sentences that describe what they see.

Reproduce the model below on an overhead so that students can see how descriptive detail enhances a piece of writing.

• Before descriptive detail:

    I'm a tall fifth-grader.

• After descriptive detail:

    I'm lanky and lean. In fact, I sometimes feel that I am mostly legs. When I fold myself into my fifth-grade desk, my feet stick out in the aisle, and my knees bump the underside of the desk.

Name _____

This Is Me!

Look in the mirror. Now look at the person sitting next to you. Eyes, ears, hair, a nose, and a mouth, right? Do you look like twins? If you have the same parts, why do you look different?

Use this page to record words and phrases that describe yourself clearly.

Hair

What is the color of your hair? Compare the color of your hair to something. Is it more the color of a daffodil, honey, butterscotch, or wheat? How long is it? How is it styled? Is it shaved, in ringlets, braided in cornrows, permed, or straight?

_____

_____

_____

Nose

Describe your nose. Think about the bridge. Is it long or short? Are your nostrils narrow or flared? Does your nose turn up? What about freckles? Sunburn?

_____

_____

_____

Eyes

Are your eyes small? Do they look soft or weepy? Are your lashes long and curved or short and thick? Think about the color and remember to compare it with something.

_____

_____

_____

Mouth

Look at your lips and your teeth. Do you have dimples? Are you smiling or frowning?

_____

_____

_____

Name _____

This Is Me!

Use the words and phrases that describe your face to write a complete description of yourself. In the box at the bottom, draw a self-portrait.

_____

_____

_____

_____

_____

Here I Am!

_____

_____

_____

_____

_____

_____

_____

_____

More Descriptive Details:
Super Sentences

One way to guarantee students will use descriptive details is to introduce them to the Super Sentence.* Using this format, students brainstorm possibilities for expanding a basic sentence and then combine the suggestions to write a super sentence.

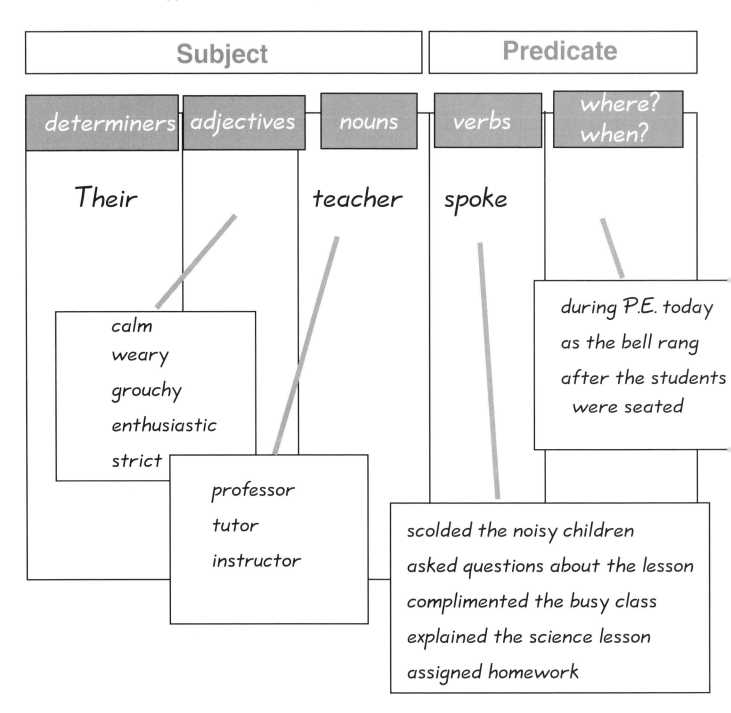

Subject			Predicate	
determiners	adjectives	nouns	verbs	where? when?
Their		teacher	spoke	

adjectives:
calm
weary
grouchy
enthusiastic
strict

nouns:
professor
tutor
instructor

verbs:
scolded the noisy children
asked questions about the lesson
complimented the busy class
explained the science lesson
assigned homework

where? when?:
during P.E. today
as the bell rang
after the students were seated

* Write a Super Sentence (EMC 205) provides 64 pages of similar lessons.

What to Do:

1. Create a chart like the sample on the left on chart paper, a transparency, or the chalkboard. Permanent charts are advantageous because they provide word banks for future writing.

2. Begin by writing a basic sentence. *Their teacher spoke.*

3. Brainstorm possible words for each category. Fill in one category at a time.

4. Create oral sentences using the words and phrases written on the chart. Guide students to make sentences that convey a clear communication. Sentences should be rich in description and still be manageable for the reader. Too many phrases without careful connections defeat the purpose of a Super Sentence.

> An unmanageable Super Sentence:
>
> *Their strict, grouchy, weary teacher scolded the noisy children on the playground by the tetherball pole during lunch recess on Monday afternoon.*
>
> A good Super Sentence:
>
> *Their weary teacher scolded the noisy children in the library yesterday.*

5. Reproduce the Super Sentence grid on page 28 for students to practice building their own Super Sentences. You might have pairs or small groups work together for several sessions before asking students to write sentences independently.

Writing Super Sentences

1. Start with a basic sentence. Add it to the chart.
2. Brainstorm. Fill in each category with describing words and phrases.
3. On the lines below, write several different sentences using the ideas on the chart.

Subject			Predicate		
determiners	adjectives	nouns	verbs	where?	when?

28

Name _____

Take a Close Look

Practice using descriptive words to write sentences that create pictures. Write about these things in your classroom.

For example:

The Door

The heavy, gray door opened to reveal a class of eager, hard-at-work students.

My Desk	

_____

_____

_____

The Chalkboard	

_____

_____

_____

The Coat Rack	

_____

_____

_____

The Trash Can	

_____

_____

_____

Name _____

Adding Details

Rewrite the following sentences, adding details to make the idea easier to picture.

For example:

Some children played.

—

Some young children played noisily on the new playground equipment.

The kitten was lost.

_____

_____

The milk was sour.

_____

_____

Dad bought a new car.

_____

_____

We made a mess.

_____

_____

My new shirt is cool.

_____

_____

Name _____

Adding Details

Rewrite the following sentences, adding details to make the idea easier to picture.

For example:

His mother called.

———

His considerate mother called when I was ill to wish me a speedy recovery.

The phone rang.

_____

_____

The butterfly flew by.

_____

_____

The baby cried.

_____

_____

I ate the cookie.

_____

_____

The puppy wagged its tail.

_____

_____

Using Figurative Language
Simile and Metaphor

When it comes to bees I'm a real chicken!

Figurative language (simile, metaphor, personification, alliteration) involves using familiar words in unfamiliar ways. Figurative language spices up sentences and makes writing more interesting.

On pages 32-33 you will find suggestions for teaching about simile and metaphor. Page 36 presents ideas for learning about personification and alliteration.

Definitions

• A simile is a figure of speech that makes a comparison using the words **like** or **as**.

> *He stood frozen, like a deer caught in the headlights of the oncoming traffic.*

• A metaphor also makes comparisons, but without using the words like or as.

> *She was a gazelle, clearing the hurdles with ease.*

Literature Models

Children's literature is a treasure chest of figurative language. Once the chest is opened, the examples spill out, sparkling in the reader's imagination. Create an awareness of this treasure among your students. Before students can use figurative language in their own writing, they need to hear many examples:

Owl Moon by Jane Yolan (Scholastic Inc., 1987) has at least one example of figurative language on almost every page.

Earthdance by Joanne Ryder (Henry Holt and Company, 1996) is written entirely in metaphor.

13 Clocks by James Thurber (Bantam, 1992) is a masterpiece of figurative language. Take the time to savor its rich use of simile and metaphor.

How Writers Use Simile and Metaphor

• To describe a character or some important action.

> In **Sootface** (Doubleday, 1994) Robert San Souci describes Sootface's hair:
>
> *"Then she combed Sootface's hair with a magic comb that made it long and thick and shiny as a blackbird's wing."*

> In the Caldecott-winning book, **Song and Dance Man** (Scholastic, 1988) Karen Ackerman describes Grandpa's dancing and singing:
>
> *"His feet move slowly at first, while his tap shoes make soft, slippery sounds like rain on a tin roof...(He) does a new step that sounds like a woodpecker tapping on a tree. Suddenly, his shoes move faster, and he begins to sing. His voice is as round and strong as a canyon echo..."*

• In an important part in the story when the author wants the reader to "see" just what is happening.

> Patricia Polacco uses them in **I Can See the Sun** (Philomel Books, 1996), just as the geese return to Lake Merritt:
>
> *"Then they heard a sound in the darkness. At first, it was a soft distant symphony of rushing wind, but it built like summer thunder, low, deep and grand."*

• In Poetry
  Read poetry and celebrate the clarity and richness of the similes and metaphors you find.

> **Snow Toward Evening** (Dial Books, 1990), a collection of twelve poems selected by Josette Frank and illustrated by Thomas Locker, is a good place to start.
>
> *"The days are short,*   *"...frost bites like a hungry shark"*
> *The sun a spark*
> *Hung thin between*   *"I wandered lonely as a cloud..."*
> *The dark and dark."*

Write Similes and Metaphors

Prewriting is important! Discuss possible comparisons, brainstorm similes and metaphors orally, then ask students to write. (Use pages 34 and 35.)

Model the use of simile and metaphor in your own journal writing. Applaud students who make meaningful comparisons in their writing.

Name _____

Using Similes

I'm as gentle as a kitten.

A simile makes a comparison by using the words **like** or **as**.

Underline the similes in the description below.

My garden was quiet under its blanket of snow. The cornstalks stood like silent sentinels. No footprints crossed the untouched whiteness. Frost decorated the fence like a lacy curtain. Winter had come, like a quiet lullaby that lulled Autumn to sleep.

List some things that you could compare to the following items.

thunder	spinach	having a tooth filled
_____	_____	_____
_____	_____	_____
_____	_____	_____
_____	_____	_____

Write a simile using each word.

1. _____

2. _____

3. _____

Name _____

Using Metaphors

Metaphors make a comparison by saying that the subject **is** something else.

> Beehives are the golden arches of a bear's life.

Identify the two things that are being compared in the metaphors below.
Write them in the box following the sentence.

The snarling dog was a flashing red light that shouted "STOP!"

My best friend, Debby, is my security blanket.

Tom snaked down the field untouched, a guided missile locked onto the goal.

Think of some interesting comparisons for the things below.
List them in the boxes.

my bedroom	recess	pizza

Use one of the comparisons to write a description below:

_____

_____

Using Figurative Language
Personification and Alliteration

My pillow is my best friend.

Personification

Personification gives animals, ideas, or inanimate objects human form and characteristics. It adds color or interest to letters, essays, and other nonfiction. Fiction writers create entire stories about animals who think, speak, and act like humans.

Find Personification in Literature

Any animal or object that takes on the characteristics of a human, or does things that a person can do, is an example of personification. Libraries are filled with wonderful examples. Start with fairy tales and picture books that your students know. Have them suggest examples.

After your class has practiced identifying personification, have a special sharing session. Students are responsible for sharing examples of personification that make the text more interesting.

> *"In the book, **Whale Brother**, Barbara Steiner personifies the moon when she says, 'He sat through the short nights when the Moon Brother painted the waters silver.' I could almost see the moon, with a giant can of silver paint, spraying the black water."*

Write Using Personification

Model the use of personification in your oral descriptions and in your own journal writing. Then encourage the students to use personification.

Page 37 provides individual practice for use after your class discussions.

Alliteration

Alliteration is the repetition of identical initial consonant sounds.

Whirling wheels whizzed by my window.

Writers use alliteration to emphasize a word, to name characters, and to add interest to their ideas.

As a class, notice alliteration in the literature that you read and practice writing alliterative descriptions. Page 38 provides individual practice in writing alliterative sentences.

Name _____

Personification

Personification gives animals, ideas, or objects human form and characteristics.

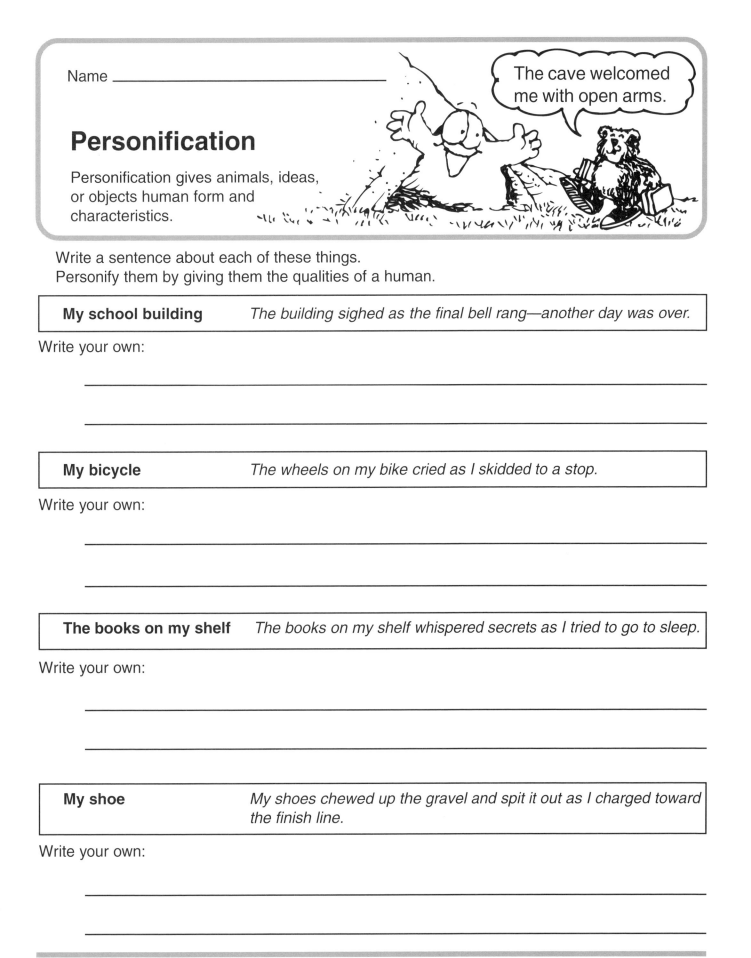

The cave welcomed me with open arms.

Write a sentence about each of these things.
Personify them by giving them the qualities of a human.

| **My school building** | *The building sighed as the final bell rang—another day was over.* |

Write your own:

_____

_____

| **My bicycle** | *The wheels on my bike cried as I skidded to a stop.* |

Write your own:

_____

_____

| **The books on my shelf** | *The books on my shelf whispered secrets as I tried to go to sleep.* |

Write your own:

_____

_____

| **My shoe** | *My shoes chewed up the gravel and spit it out as I charged toward the finish line.* |

Write your own:

_____

_____

Name _____

Suddenly soapy suds seemed to swallow my sweater.

Using Alliteration

Alliteration is the repetition of initial identical consonant sounds.

Use the words below in sentences that have alliteration.

baby
dozens
mud
fly

What Is a Paragraph?

Before students can write a good paragraph, they must understand paragraph structure. A paragraph has two essential components:

- a main idea expressed in a topic sentence and

- additional sentences providing supporting details.

Pages 40-41 provide activities to help your students to identify the parts of paragraph.

1. Provide many experiences in recognizing the **main idea** of a paragraph and the **topic sentence** that expresses it.

    - Read sample paragraphs from text or literature books. Have students locate the main ideas and topic sentences.

    - Read samples from students' work. Have them determine if there is a clear main idea and if it is expressed in a topic sentence. With students' permission, prepare samples as overhead transparencies and use them with the whole class.

    - Use the sample paragraphs on pages 42-44 to practice identifying the main idea and the topic sentence.

2. Practice identifying sentences that contain **details that support the topic sentence**. These sentences give additional information, helping the reader to understand the paragraph's main idea.

    Sample paragraphs from literature, student work, and pages 45-47 can be used for this practice.

3. Once students have become proficient at identifying the topic sentence and supporting details in a paragraph, ask them to read sample paragraphs and to **eliminate any details that do not relate to the main idea** and therefore should not be included in the paragraph.

    The sample paragraphs on pages 48-49 contain extraneous information that should be eliminated to create good paragraphs.

Recognizing the Main Idea

The reproducible practice paragraphs on the bottom of this page and on page 41 are of graduated difficulty. Select those that are appropriate for your students.

What's the point?

1. Make transparencies or reproduce the sample paragraphs. Have students tell the main idea in each paragraph.

2. Then ask students to identify the sentence that states that main idea. Explain that this sentence is called the **topic sentence** of the paragraph.

Note: This is a good pair-share activity. Each individual reads the paragraph and determines the topic sentence independently. Then the partners compare answers and together explain why an answer was chosen.

Remember main ideas may be stated in several different ways.

Main Idea

Teeth have three important jobs. First, they chew. They break food into small pieces and make it easier to swallow. Teeth are for talking, too. Front teeth help people say special sounds like the *th* in toothbrush. Teeth also help support the muscles around the mouth. They help to give a face its shape.

Main Idea

Lantern fish live near the bottom of the ocean where it is very dark, so they carry their own lights. The lights look like tiny glowing pearls. They are called photophores. A lantern fish can flash its photophores on and off. A lantern fish gives off enough light to light up a dark room.

Main Idea

A backswimmer has a rounded back and its underside is flat. When it floats on its back it looks like a little boat. It rows itself along in the water using its two hind legs like oars. The backswimmer spends most of its time upside down.

Main Idea

When Martin Luther King, Jr. spoke, people listened. Poor people, rich people, white people, black people, people from other countries —they all listened. Many helped him work, march, sing, and pray for justice. He asked people not to fight with each other. He suggested peaceful ways to solve problems. Martin Luther King, Jr. had a special talent for leadership.

Name _____

Find the Main Idea

Read each paragraph.

Write the main idea on the line.

Draw a line under the topic sentence.

Be ready to tell why you picked that sentence.

The centipede is a hunter. It poisons its prey with a quick bite. It stalks its prey in dark places beneath stones, logs, and piles of leaves. It eats silverfish, cockroaches, worms, and slugs.

Main Idea: _____

Charlie McCarthy was a wooden dummy. He was owned by the famous ventriloquist, Edgar Bergen. Mr. Bergen created Charlie while he was in high school. Charlie traveled around the world with Mr. Bergen. They performed for many people. Charlie was so popular that he got more mail than Mr. Bergen did. Even a puppet can be a famous star.

Main Idea: _____

When water is forced upward through sand, by a natural spring or some other source, the grains of sand are pushed apart and the sand swells. When this happens, the sand is no longer firm and cannot support heavy weight. It becomes quicksand. If the water drains or stops running, the quicksand turns back into plain sand. So quicksand is not a special kind of sand, it is the result of water trying to move through plain old sand.

Main Idea: _____

Name _____

Find the Main Idea

Read each paragraph.

Write the main idea on the line.

Draw a line under the topic sentence.

Be ready to tell why you picked that sentence.

It takes a week to make a jelly bean. First, a mixture of water, cornstarch, sugar, and corn syrup is made. Flavorings are added and the mixture is cooled and poured into tiny molds. After the centers harden, they are given a steam bath and a sugar shower. Then colored syrup is poured over each center and allowed to harden into a hard shell. Last, the shell is polished. Seven days have gone by and the jelly beans are finally ready for eating.

Main Idea: _____

Next time you see lightning, count the number of seconds that pass until you hear the thunder. The lightning is a mile away for every five seconds that you count. In this way, you can "measure" how far the lightning is from you. Scientists know that the speed of light is faster than the speed of sound. So calculating the difference between the two speeds, they have developed this easy five-second formula.

Main Idea: _____

During parties in Mexico, children are blindfolded and given a stick. They use the stick to try to break a piñata. The piñata, a decorated container filled with candy and small treats, is an important festival tradition. Piñatas are made in many shapes. The special containers are suspended by ropes. As the children take turns trying to hit the piñata, the rope is used to raise and lower it, to make breaking it even harder. When the piñata is broken, all of the children scramble for the goodies that spill on the floor.

Main Idea: _____

Name _____

Find the Main Idea

Read each paragraph.

Write the main idea on the line.

Draw a line under the topic sentence.

Be ready to tell why you picked that sentence.

The air all around us is filled with water vapor. When it is heated, water changes from a liquid form into an invisible gas called water vapor. When the water vapor in the air cools, it turns back into tiny droplets of water to form a cloud. The same water moves from liquid form to water vapor and back to liquid form over and over again. This pattern of change is called the water cycle.

Main Idea: _____

In 1903, Orville Wright was the pilot and only passenger in a biplane that he and his brother had built. The flight took place in Kittyhawk, North Carolina, on a sandy stretch of beach. The plane looked like a giant box kite. The flight lasted only twelve seconds, but that twelve seconds marked the beginning of a new era in transportation - travel by air.

Main Idea: _____

Jesse Owens was the son of Alabama sharecroppers. As a child he was skinny and often sick. When he was nine, his family moved to Ohio to find a better life. It was there, while Jesse was in junior high school, that he met his mentor, Charles Riley, a gym teacher and coach of the track team. Coach Riley taught Jesse to run and jump. Jesse set his first track and field record in that junior high. He went on to set records in high school, college, and the Olympic Games. Jesse Owens, sometimes called the World's Fastest Human, began life as a poor sharecropper's son and became a world hero.

Main Idea: _____

Name _____

Find the Supporting Details

Read each paragraph.

Underline the topic sentence.

Write the main idea.

List two supporting details under the main idea.

Feathers have three parts. The shaft is the stiff part in the middle. The shaft has barbs sticking out from each side. The barbs have little "hairs" called filaments sticking out of them. The end of each filament is a tiny hook to keep it in place.

Main Idea: _____

Details:

1. _____

2. _____

Wolves are hungry hunters. To stay alive, they need lots of fresh meat. A hungry wolf can eat twenty pounds of meat at a single meal. Because of their huge appetites, wolves usually hunt big animals like deer and moose. But a hungry wolf will chase and eat smaller prey like a rabbit or a mouse too. It may even go fishing.

Main Idea: _____

Details:

1. _____

2. _____

Note: See the teaching ideas on page 39.

Name _____

Find the Supporting Details

Read each paragraph.

Underline the topic sentence.

Write the main idea.

List two supporting details under the main idea.

Some seeds move on the wind. They have wing-like parts to catch the wind. Other seeds have hooks or stickers. They catch in the fur of animals and are carried to new places. Some seeds float on water to new places. People move seeds too. They plant them in their yards and gardens. Seeds travel in many different ways.

Main Idea: _____

Details:

1. _____

2. _____

According to nutritionists, and Winnie-the-Pooh, honey is a very useful food. It is good for active people because it gives them energy. It is a natural sugar, and nutritionists recommend natural foods. Honey is almost twice as sweet as sugar so it is an excellent sweetener. When you use honey in cooking, it keeps food moist and adds a flavor of its own.

Main Idea: _____

Details:

1. _____

2. _____

Name _____

Find the Supporting Details

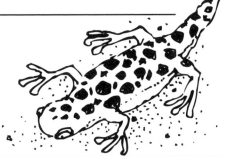

Read the paragraph.

Underline the topic sentence.

Write the main idea.

List three supporting details under the main idea.

The spotted salamander remains almost unchanged from the first salamander that walked on the earth about 330 million years ago. It lives in caves, under rocks and logs, and only moves during the blackest hours of the night. It eats insects and worms and lives in the earthen darkness, just as its early ancestors did. Its soft legs, clawless toes, and moist body look just like those of generations of salamanders that have come before it. Its eyes peer into the darkness, but they do not move like other creatures' eyes. It only sees things that move. It cannot see things that are still. It "hears" with primitive ears that lay inside its head and along its body and tail. Once a year, on the night of the first spring rain after the first spring thaw, it visits a woodland pond, the same pond that its ancestors visited, to lay its eggs. Then it returns to the darkness of its home in the moist earth of the forest.

Main Idea: _____

Details:

    1. _____

    2. _____

    3. _____

What Doesn't Belong?

Name _____

Read the paragraphs below.

Each one contains a sentence that doesn't belong.

When you find it, draw a line under it.

Be ready to tell why it shouldn't be in the paragraph.

The hummingbird is like a helicopter. It can fly up. It can fly down. It can fly forward and backward. It can even hover in one place. Just as the rotors of the helicopter spin very fast, the wings of a hummingbird flap over eighty times in one second. Hummingbirds can barely walk.

My little brother drives me crazy. He has red hair and blue eyes. Whenever I have a friend over, he wants to play with us. When I need to do homework, he races through the house like a fire engine. When my family goes for a ride in the car, he has to sit by the window. Talking on the phone when he's around is a real challenge. He always wants to say "hello." When I complain, Mom and Dad always take his side - "After all, he's only four years old." I can't wait until he's five!

The Apollo Project was a project announced by President Kennedy in 1961. Its goal was to land a man on the moon. Scientists worked hard for eight years to achieve this goal. After many preliminary flights, Neil Armstrong stepped onto the moon's surface. On July 20, 1969, he and his fellow astronaut, Edwin Aldrin, landed in the lunar module, while Michael Collins controlled the Apollo spacecraft, which continued in orbit around the moon. They took samples of lunar rocks and brought them back to Earth in Apollo 11. Today space shuttles routinely take off and return to the Earth on various space missions.

What Doesn't Belong?

Read the paragraphs below.

Each one contains a sentence that doesn't belong.

When you find it, draw a line under it.

Be ready to tell why it shouldn't be in the paragraph.

Morse Code is an international code for transmitting messages by wire or radio using signals of short and long duration. Short signals are called dots and long signals called dashes. The code was originated by Samuel Morse for use on his telegraph. The letters SOS (three short signals, three long signals, three short signals) are an international distress signal. By radio telephone the distress call is "Mayday."

Birthdays are important events at my house. Halloween is fun too. Everyone in the family joins in wishing the birthday person the best. There's a huge dinner with special food. The birthday person gets to use the red birthday plate. Of course, there's also a cake and candles and singing, followed by presents - one for each year. But the best part is the feeling of being a family and knowing that you are surrounded by love.

Where do you sleep? Animals sleep in many different places. Horses and giraffes sleep standing up. Bats sleep upside down. Fish and snakes sleep with their eyes open. Some birds use special muscles to lock their claws to the branches so that they can perch on the branch without falling as they sleep. Cats sleep as much as twenty hours a day. Hippos sleep in a big heap. I sleep in a comfortable, soft, cozy, warm bed and I'm glad that I do!

Writing Supporting Details

Pages 51-53 provide practice in writing details to support a stated main idea. Writing supporting details is usually easier for students than developing a topic sentence. However, students sometimes need help in learning to leave out information that doesn't support the stated main idea. You may want to review some of the paragraphs on pages 48 and 49 before introducing the lessons in this section.

Guided Paragraph Completion

1. Choose a topic that relates to a recent area of study in your classroom.

   - Write a topic sentence on the chalkboard that addresses the topic.

   - Have students list information that would support the topic sentence.

   - Read the completed list with your students. Evaluate whether each detail listed supports the topic sentence. Cross out any information that students agree is unnecessary.

   - Ask students to write a paragraph that includes the topic sentence and some of the supporting details that they have listed.

2. Repeat this lesson format until you feel students are ready for independent practice using the reproducible worksheets on pages 51-53.

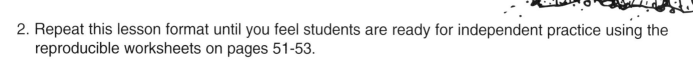

50   Writing Fabulous Sentences & Paragraphs EMC 575

Note: See teaching ideas on page 50.

Name _____

Write Supporting Details

Read the topic sentences.
Write three supporting details for each one.

Breakfast is an important meal.

1._____

2._____

3._____

Learning happens on the playground, as well as in the classroom.

1._____

2._____

3._____

Animals communicate in many ways.

1._____

2._____

3._____

Note: See teaching ideas on page 50.

Name _____

Write Supporting Details

Read the topic sentences.
Write three supporting details for each one.

Computers are important tools for learning.

1. _____

2. _____

3. _____

Exercise helps keep you healthy.

1. _____

2. _____

3. _____

Voting in elections is an important responsibility.

1. _____

2. _____

3. _____

Name _____

Write Supporting Details

Read the topic sentences.
Write three supporting details for each one.

Hiking is fun.

1._____

2._____

3._____

Thomas Edison made my life easier.

1._____

2._____

3._____

The way you look is important.

1._____

2._____

3._____

Writing Topic Sentences

A good topic sentence is essential for a good paragraph. Help students write topic sentences that are specific to the information included in their paragraphs.

A Main Idea May Be Stated in Several Different Ways

Help students realize that there can be more than one appropriate topic sentence for a specific paragraph. This activity is a valuable prewriting experience for students as they begin to write their own paragraphs.

1. Put a topic and a set of details on the chalkboard or make a chart or transparency. (Sample sets are included on page 55. Cover up the topic until your students have discussed the details.)

2. Read the details with your students.

3. Discuss what the details have in common.

4. Have the students think of sentences that describe this commonality. The commonality is the main idea.

5. Brainstorm ways to say this main idea in the form of a sentence. Be sure to acknowledge that the main idea may be expressed in several different topic sentences.

6. When the discussion has been completed, let each student select one of the topic sentences suggested by the group and write a paragraph containing the information provided in the "details" list.

7. Pages 56-59 provide additional practice in selecting and writing topic sentences.

Examples for the teacher:

Main Idea - **Parts of a Hand**

Possible Topic Sentences -

   The hand has five different parts that help it function.

   The hand is made up of many different parts.

   Different parts working together help my hand to move and feel.

Main idea - **A Picnic**

Possible Topic Sentences -

   There are lots of things to do when you get ready to go on a picnic.

   Going on a picnic means packing a variety of supplies.

   Another name for a picnic might be "Pack and Go."

Parts of a Hand

- 8 small bones
- ligaments to hold the bones together
- nerves that help you feel things
- muscles to move
- blood

Valentina Tereshkova

- Russian cosmonaut
- first woman in space — January 16, 1963
- three day flight
- airline pilot
- parachutes for hobby

A Picnic

- pack the food
- get the fishing poles
- find blankets and folding chairs
- fill the cooler with ice
- load in the car

Friends

- companion
- support
- always there
- someone you care about
- someone who shares

Ben Franklin

- research on electricity
- invented lightning rod
- invented free-standing, wood-burning stove
- organized U.S. postal system
- wrote *Poor Richard's Almanac*

The Sun

- closest star to Earth
- ball of burning gases
- source of heat and light
- 70% hydrogen 30% helium
- about 4.7 billion years old

Name _____

Putting It All Together 1

Read the topic and the details below.

Think of a topic sentence about the golden eagle.

Write it down.

Write sentences that support the topic sentence and include the details given.

Golden Eagle

- large, heavy hooked bill
- strong, sharp claws called talons
- brown with golden tints on the head and back of the neck
- feathers on the legs all the way to their talons
- majestic looking
- wide wing span

My Paragraph About the Golden Eagle

_____

_____

_____

_____

_____

_____

Name _____

Putting It All Together 2

Read the topic and the details below.

Think of a topic sentence about Louisa May Alcott.

Write it down.

Write sentences that support the topic sentence and include the details given.

Louisa May Alcott

- born November 29, 1832
- lived most of life in Concord, Massachusetts
- one of four sisters
- didn't have much money
- became a successful author

My Paragraph About Louisa May Alcott

_____

_____

_____

_____

_____

_____

Name _____

Putting It All Together 3

Read the topic and the details below.

Think of a topic sentence about elephants.

Write it down.

Write sentences that support the topic sentence and include the details given.

Elephants

- weigh about 8 tons
- thick, gray, wrinkled skin
- large head
- long trunk
- tusks

My Paragraph About Elephants

_____

_____

_____

_____

_____

_____

Name _____

Putting It All Together 4

Read the topic and the details below.

Think of a topic sentence about soccer.

Write it down.

Write sentences that support the topic sentence and include the details given.

Soccer

- originated in United Kingdom
- played by two eleven-player teams
- large rectangular field
- object of the game—to send the ball, with the feet or head, into opponents' goal

My Paragraph About Soccer

_____

_____

_____

_____

_____

_____

_____

Forms to Organize Writing

As students begin to write paragraphs, using forms to organize information will ensure success. Pages 61-78 provide reproducible writing forms that serve various purposes:

Purpose of Paragraph	Type of Paragraph	Forms Found on:
give directions	How-to Paragraphs	(pages 61-64)
tell a story	Narrative Paragraphs	(pages 65-68)
compare different things	Compare/Contrast Paragraphs	(pages 69-71)
describe an event or an object	Descriptive Paragraphs	(pages 72-74)
argue for a certain position	Persuasive Paragraphs	(pages 75-76)
define a term	Definition Paragraphs	(pages 77-78)

Model the use of the organizer forms in guided lessons before you expect your students to use the forms independently.

Using Paragraph Forms as Guided Lessons

1. Give each student a copy of a form. Talk about the purpose of the paragraph.

2. Brainstorm and list responses to the first blank space on the form.

3. Have each student select one response from the list to copy on the form.

4. Continue until each part of the form has been filled in.

5. Ask students to share their completed paragraphs.

Using Paragraph Forms for Independent Practice

1. Give each student a copy of the form.

2. Go through the steps required in the assignment. Be sure students understand the purpose of the paragraph.

3. Develop a word bank for student writing by brainstorming possible words and phrases that might be used in the paragraph. Write these on the chalkboard.

4. Students work independently to fill in the form and to write their own paragraphs.

Note: Each form contains a "bonus" activity at the bottom. These can be covered up before reproducing if you do not wish to use them.

Name _____

How to Clean a Room

Organizer
for a
How-To
Paragraph

Have you ever had to clean your room? I've developed this

procedure that I follow when I clean mine. First, I _____

_____. Next, I

_____.

It's important to _____

_____, too. Finally, I

_____

and I'm finished.

Write More About It

Think of another job that you do.
List the steps you have to follow.

Name _____

Cleaning the Cage

YUK

Organizer for a **How-To** Paragraph

Having a pet _____ can be a lot of fun, but

cleaning the cage is a lot of work. First I have to _____

_____

Next I _____

Then I _____

Finally I _____

Now my _____ needs cleaning too.

Write More About It

Pretend that you have to send invitations for your birthday party. Give at least three steps that you have to follow.

Note: See teaching ideas on page 60.

Name _____

An Ice-Cream Sundae

Organizer
for a
How-To
Paragraph

Making an ice-cream sundae is a sweet job. Here's how I do

it. First I _____

Second I _____

Third I _____

Then I _____

I can't wait to eat!

Write More About It

Packing a lunch is an important job. List the
steps that you have to follow when you
pack yours.

63

Note: See teaching ideas on page 60.

Name ______________________

Write your topic here:

Organizer for a **How-To** Paragraph

List the how-to steps here:

______________________ ______________________

______________________ ______________________

______________________ ______________________

Choose a topic sentence:

____

____

Now, write your how-to paragraph.

____

____

____

____

____

____

____

Note: See teaching ideas on page 60.

Name _____

The Most Important Day of My Life

Organizer for a **Narrative** Paragraph

Most of my days follow a similar pattern, but there was one day that was different. It was the day I _____

_____.

I think that it was the most important day of my life. It all started when_____

_____

_____

When it was over I knew_____

_____

Write More About It

Describe the everyday pattern of your days.

Most of my days follow a similar pattern...

Writing Fabulous Sentences & Paragraphs EMC 575

Note: See teaching ideas on page 60.

Name _____

A Terrible No-Good Day

Organizer
for a
Narrative
Paragraph

Yesterday was a terrible, no-good day. I felt awful. It all

started when _____

_____

_____

Then _____

_____

The last straw was when _____.

_____

Tomorrow has got to be better.

Write More About It

Write a paragraph about one of these feelings:

fear   embarrassment   pride   happiness   anger

Note: See teaching ideas on page 60.

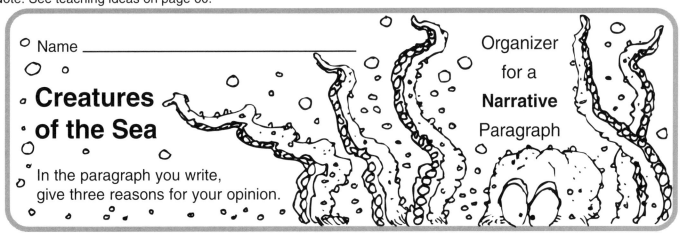

Name _____

Creatures of the Sea

In the paragraph you write, give three reasons for your opinion.

Organizer for a **Narrative** Paragraph

In my opinion the most unusual creature of the sea is a...

_____

_____

_____

_____

_____

_____

_____

_____

_____

Write More About It

Write another paragraph about another sea creature. Be sure that your paragraph has a topic sentence and three or more supporting details.

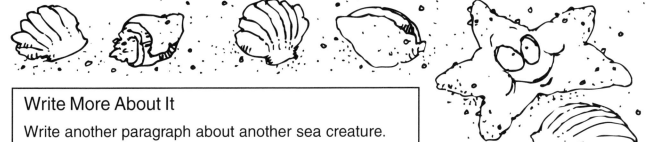

Name _____

Party Time

Organizer for a **Narrative** Paragraph

The best party that I've ever been to was _____

_____

_____

Everyone had to _____

_____

_____

Then we _____

_____

_____

Best of all, _____

_____

_____

I didn't want the party to end.

Write More About It

Write about the worst party you ever attended.

Name _____

Pilgrims to a New Land

Organizer

for a

Compare/Contrast

Paragraph

The Pilgrims who came to America on the Mayflower and modern day immigrants who come to America from other countries lived during different times, but they shared hopes and dreams.

I think that the most important dream that they share is…

_____

_____

_____

_____

_____

_____

_____

_____

Write More About It

Write two or more supporting sentences for this topic sentence…

The people who come to America today have very different lives than those who came in 1600.

Name _____

Whales and Sharks

Organizer
for a
Compare/Contrast
Paragraph

Whales and sharks are alike in several ways. They both

_____

_____

_____

_____

They also _____

_____

_____

_____

Finally _____

_____

_____

Write More About It
Now write a paragraph that explains how whales and sharks are different.

Name _____

Organizer

for a

Compare/Contrast

Paragraph

I will write about _____ and _____.
first thing   second thing

List similarities:

_____

_____

_____

List differences:

_____

_____

_____

Topic Sentence:

_____

_____

My paragraph:

_____

_____

_____

_____

_____

_____

_____

_____

Name _____

Yum!
Yum!

Organizer
for a
Descriptive
Paragraph

The very best food in the world is _____

_____

(Describe how it looks)

_____

_____

(Describe how it smells)

_____

_____

(Describe how it tastes)

_____

_____

You should try it some time. You might like it too!

Write More About It

Write a paragraph about your favorite dessert, snack, party food, or sandwich.
Describe how it looks, smells, and tastes. Explain why you think someone else should try it.

Name _____

My Room

Organizer

for a

Descriptive

Paragraph

My room is my own special place. When you step inside, you will notice…

_____

_____

_____

_____

_____

_____

_____

_____

Come and visit anytime.

Please KNOCK !!

Write More About It

Write about another place that you like to be.

Name _____

Loud Learning!

Give three examples of noisy learning.

Organizer
for a
Descriptive
Paragraph

Learning is sometimes a noisy activity. _____

_____

_____

_____

_____

_____

_____

_____

_____

Be prepared to wear ear plugs and join me.

Write More About It

Write about how learning is quiet. Include at least three examples.

Note: See teaching ideas on page 60.

Name _____

Organizer
for a
Persuasive
Paragraph

Which are you?

Tall Is Terrific

Being tall is terrific. One of the advantages is _____

_____

Another is _____

_____

Finally _____

_____

Won't you join the touters of tall?

Small Is Swell!

Being small is terrific. One of the advantages is _____

_____

Another is _____

_____

Finally _____

_____

Won't you join the proponents of small?

Writing Fabulous Sentences & Paragraphs EMC 575

Name _____

I Vote for Computers

Organizer
for a
Persuasive
Paragraph

Computers are important to my future because _____

_____

_____

_____

_____

I know that they will help _____

_____

_____

_____

_____

I am glad that I can use computers.

Write More About It

Choose something that you think is important.
Try to convince your readers that they should recognize the importance.

Note: See teaching ideas on page 60.

Name _____

Recess

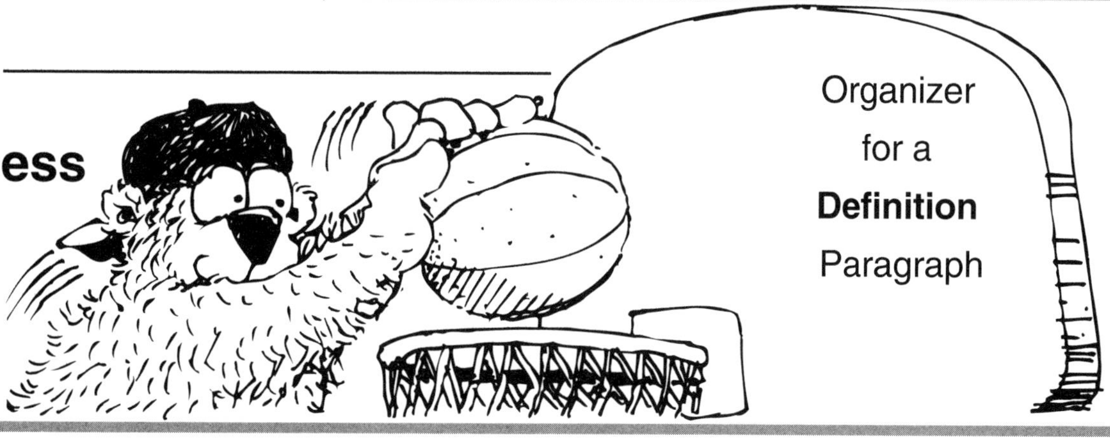

Organizer
for a
Definition
Paragraph

Recess is _____

_____

_____

Some people believe that _____

_____

_____

but I know _____

_____

_____

Recess is _____

_____

_____

Write More About It

Write a paragraph that defines your favorite recess activity.

Name _____

Friendship

Topic and Organizer

for a

Definition

Paragraph

What is friendship? Well, I have discovered that friendship

It is_____

That's what friendship is.

Write More About It

You have defined friendship; what implications does that have for being a friend?
Write another paragraph defining a friend.

Paragraph Organization

Learning That Paragraphs Are Important

Paragraphs help the reader to understand what an author is saying. Just as it is easier to find a can of soup in a cupboard that is carefully organized, it is easier to find the premise of a story or report if the sentences are organized into paragraphs.

Let your students draw this conclusion themselves by doing this exercise with them.

1. Reproduce pages 81 and 82. Both selections include exactly the same sentences.

2. Give students the page 81 and read the passage together. Then hand out page 82. Have them compare the unorganized writing and the organized writing.

   • Which piece is easier to read?

   • Which piece is easier to understand?

   • In which piece would it be easier to locate specific information?

Organizing Sentences into Paragraphs

Learning to organize information into paragraphs is a difficult yet extremely important skill. A model whole-class lesson and two independent small group or individual practice activities are provided.

The Model Lesson

Before you begin:

- Reproduce pages 83-85 on transparencies or a chart.
- Cut the sentences apart.

Modeling the process:

- Explain to your class that you have written a report on Native Americans, but that the report is not organized. Read the sentences together.
- Guide students to generate general categories of information that would be the main ideas of each paragraph. (For example: life before Europeans arrived, how they became known as "Indians," life after the Europeans arrived, Native Americans today.)
- Make a "basket" for each category.
- Read each sentence of the report and let students decide in which basket it should be placed.
- When all sentences have been distributed, explain that each basket will represent a paragraph in your written report. Dump out one basket at a time and work with students to put the sentences in a readable order. Then copy the sentences into a paragraph.

Individual Practice

Pages 86-89 provide practice for small groups or individual students in organizing sentences into cohesive paragraphs.

Organizing Lists of Facts into Paragraphs

After your students have practiced organizing sentences into paragraphs, move on to organizing a list of facts and then writing paragraphs after the details have been organized.

Pages 90-92 provide lists of facts for this activity. These pages can be reproduced on an overhead transparency or on paper depending on how you decide to conduct the lessons.

Steps to follow:

1. Read the facts.
2. Group the facts into categories.* (You might want to use the multi-section web form on page 99.) The category will be the topic or main idea of the paragraph.
3. Think of sentences that describe the commonalities of each group of facts (topic sentences.)
4. For each paragraph, use the sentence as the topic sentence and write the supporting details including the facts from the category.

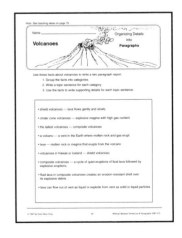

* As you guide students in categorizing the facts, don't comment on incorrect placement immediately. Let students discover where changes are needed.

Name _____

An Unorganized Report

Engineers of the Pond

Beavers are interesting animals because they change the habitat in which they live. Beavers do this by blocking up streams to create ponds. Then they build their homes, called lodges, in these ponds. Beavers' bodies make them well-suited for underwater building. Special muscles close off their noses, ears, and throats to keep the water out. Beavers' broad tails act like rudders for steering. Their two very large, orange front teeth are used to gnaw down trees. They begin building their dam from the side of the stream, moving out toward the center. Stones are rolled and pushed on top of the limbs and branches to keep the wood from floating away. When a beaver builds a dam, everyone in the family helps. Beavers use their front paws to scoop mud from the bottom to fill in the spaces. Beavers can stay underwater for fifteen minutes while they are working. Their webbed back feet make them excellent swimmers. Strong front paws with claws help them dig and carry. Mother, father, and three or four younger beavers work together. First they cut trees down with their big, strong teeth. Next they gnaw them into smaller sections and drag them into the water. When the dam is completed, a pond will form behind it. The beavers will continue to check for leaks and repair the dam as needed. They have see-through eyelids that act like goggles so they can see well as they swim beneath the surface. They are now ready to start work on the dome-shaped lodge that will be their home in the pond. The lodge looks like a giant pile of sticks from the outside. It is hollow inside, with a ledge above the water level. The entrance is under the water.

Note: See teaching ideas on page 79.

Name _____

An Organized Report

Engineers of the Pond

Beavers are interesting animals because they change the habitat in which they live. Beavers do this by blocking up streams to create ponds. Then they build their homes, called lodges, in these ponds.

Beavers' bodies make them well-suited for underwater building. Special muscles close off their noses, ears, and throats to keep the water out. Beavers can stay underwater for fifteen minutes while they are working. They have see-through eyelids that act like goggles so they can see well as they swim beneath the surface.

Beavers' broad tails act like rudders for steering. Their webbed back feet make them excellent swimmers. Strong front paws with claws help them dig and carry. Their two, very large orange front teeth are used to gnaw down trees.

When a beaver builds a dam, everyone in the family helps. Mother, Father, and three or four younger beavers work together. First they cut trees down with their big, strong teeth. Next they gnaw them into smaller sections and drag them into the water.

They begin building their dam from the side of the stream, moving out toward the center. Stones are rolled and pushed on top of the limbs and branches to keep the wood from floating away. Beavers use their front paws to scoop mud from the bottom to fill in the spaces.

When the dam is completed, a pond will form behind it. The beavers will continue to check for leaks and repair the dam as needed. They are now ready to start work on the dome-shaped lodge that will be their home in the pond. The lodge looks like a giant pile of sticks from the outside. It is hollow inside, with a ledge above the water level. The entrance is under the water.

 Writing Fabulous Sentences and Paragraphs EMC 575

Note: See teaching ideas on page 79-80.

The First Americans

Several million people lived in North America before the arrival of Europeans.

The Native Americans called themselves by the names of their tribes.

The history of the Native Americans following the Europeans' discovery of America is a story of hardship.

When the United States became an independent nation, the government started moving the Native Americans off their land and giving it to the white settlers.

Native Americans believed that the land was for everyone to use and share.

There were hundreds of tribes in America when Christopher Columbus arrived and thought that he was in India.

The Europeans brought many sicknesses with them that the Native Americans had never seen.

83   *Writing Fabulous Sentences and Paragraphs EMC 575*

By the late 1800s most Native Americans were forced to live on reservations.

As citizens of their tribal nations, they take part in their tribal government and can choose to live on or off their tribal lands.

Some of the people were hunters and others were farmers.

The hunters moved across the land killing only the animals that they needed for food, tools, clothing, and shelter.

Columbus called all of the tribes "Indians" even though the people that he referred to were scattered all over the country, spoke different languages, and had different customs.

The Europeans wanted to take over and claim the new land as theirs.

Today there are hundreds of reservations located in thirty-four states.

Many Native Americans live on these reservations.

They proudly hold onto their tribal customs and teach the history of their people to their children.

Other Native Americans live in cities and towns across the United States.

In 1924, the Snyder Act made all Native Americans citizens of the United States.

So today Native Americans are members of two groups.

As citizens of the United States, they vote, pay taxes, and serve in the military.

Some Europeans wanted the Native Americans to change the ways in which they lived.

A Historical Perspective

Cut the sentences on these two pages apart and arrange them into three paragraphs. The first sentence of each paragraph is numbered to help you get started.

(1) For over 100 years, students and teachers in the United States have begun their school day with a special salute to America and its flag.

How did these patriotic practices begin?

(1) The original Pledge of Allegiance was written by Francis Bellamy.

They recite the Pledge of Allegiance and sing a patriotic song like "The Star-Spangled Banner."

(1) From a boat in Baltimore Harbor, Francis Scott Key observed the British bombing of Fort McHenry in the War of 1812.

During the night, he saw only glimpses of the American flag through the smoke and the flares of light.

He wrote it to honor the 400th anniversary of Columbus's voyage to America.

The next morning, he was so happy to see the flag still flying that he began writing a poem.

It appeared in a children's magazine in 1892 and a month later was recited in public schools in celebration of Columbus Day.

Later, this poem was put to the tune of another song and became America's national anthem, "The Star-Spangled Banner."

Note: See teaching ideas on pages 79 and 80.

Bat Facts

Cut the sentences on these two pages apart and arrange them into three paragraphs. The first sentence of each paragraph is numbered to help you get started.

(1) All bats belong to a group of animals called mammals.

When the bat hears the echoes, it knows how far away something is.

(1) The 1,000 different species of bats are divided into two main groups: megabats and microbats.

While they are young, their mothers feed them with milk.

When the sound waves hit something, they bounce back as echoes.

In fact, bats make up nearly one-fourth of the world's mammals.

Mammals have fur and their babies are born alive.

(1) Bats are nocturnal creatures and fly at night.

The megabats live in tropical regions and eat mostly fruit.

Bats' bodies are covered with fur and baby bats do not hatch from eggs; they are born alive like puppies and kittens.

They use "echolocation" to navigate through dark caves and forests.

Microbats are small and mainly eat insects - as many as 3,000 in one night.

As a bat flies, it makes high-pitched sounds. The sounds spread through the air in waves.

Note: See teaching ideas on page 79.

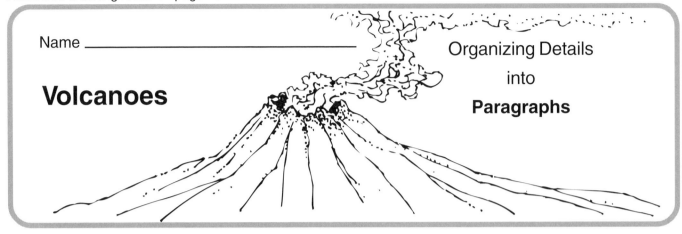

Name _____

Volcanoes

Organizing Details

into

Paragraphs

Use these facts about volcanoes to write a two paragraph report.

    1. Group the facts into categories.

    2. Write a topic sentence for each category.

    3. Use the facts to write supporting details for each topic sentence.

- shield volcanoes — gently sloping sides; erupt quietly; lava flows gently and slowly, spreads a long way

- cinder cone volcanoes — steep-sided, but relatively small

- composite volcanoes — the tallest volcanoes

- a volcano — a vent in the Earth where molten rock and gas erupt

- lava — molten rock or magma that erupts from the volcano

- volcanoes in Hawaii or Iceland — shield volcanoes

- composite volcanoes — a cycle of quiet eruptions of fluid lava followed by explosive eruptions

- fluid lava in composite volcanoes creates an erosion-resistant shell over its explosive debris

- cinder cone volcanoes — explosive magma with high gas content; lava bombs blow high into air

- lava can flow out of vent as liquid or explode from vent as solid or liquid particles

Writing Fabulous Sentences & Paragraphs EMC 575

Name _____

Prairie Dogs

Organizing Details
into
Paragraphs

Use these facts about prairie dogs to write a two paragraph report.

    1. Group the facts into categories.

    2. Write a topic sentence for each category.

    3. Use the facts to write supporting details for each topic sentence.

- stout-bodied

- ground-dwelling

- member of squirrel family

- native to prairies and other open, grassy areas

- short legs

- short tail

- small ears

- live in family groups called coteries

- grizzled, yellowish to reddish gray or brown coat

- bark-like yip

- several coteries form a ward

- towns contain thousands of individuals

- weigh between 1 and 3 pounds (700 g to 1.4 kg)

- wards are united into a town

- town — a complex system of underground, interconnecting burrows

Ice Cream

Organizing Details
into
Paragraphs

Name _____

Use these facts about ice cream to write a two paragraph report.

1. Group the facts into categories.

2. Write a topic sentence for each category.

3. Use the facts to write supporting details for each topic sentence.

- mixture of cream, milk, sweetener, flavoring, and air

- popular frozen food

- Marco Polo brought recipe for frozen milk dessert to Italy from Far East — 1295

- first ice cream factory in Baltimore — 1851

- United States — consume 14 quarts per person annually

- air beaten into milk mixture as it freezes

- Italy credited with popularizing

- United States — biggest ice cream eaters

- many flavors

Planning Paragraphs Using a Web

A web is an organizational method that displays ideas in an easily visible form.

- Students who are unfamiliar with webs will need to begin with the simple one-section web (pages 95-97).

- More experienced writers can use multi-section webs to write a report or story with more than one paragraph (pages 98-99).

One-Section Webs

Use the simple one-step web form on page 95 to introduce the use of webs as a planning device.

- Reproduce the web on a transparency or draw it on the chalkboard. Explain what each oval contains.
  (Center oval - main idea; outside ovals - supporting details.)

- As a class, use the web to write a paragraph together.

  1. Develop possible topic sentences about the main idea in the center oval.

  2. Suggest possible sentences about the supporting details in the outside ovals.

  3. Write the paragraph.

Reproduce pages 96 and 97 for independent practice.

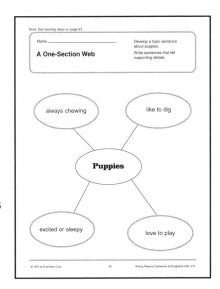

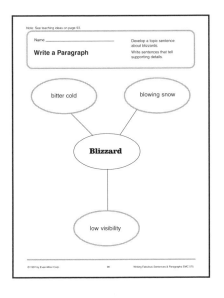

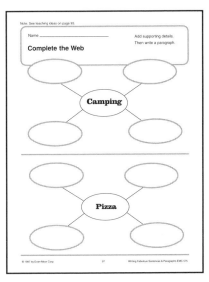

Multi-Section Webs

A web can contain many sections, with each section setting up the main idea and supporting ideas for a paragraph.

Introducing multi-section webs:

- Make a transparency of the multi-section web form on page 98 to show your students how such a web can be used.

- After reading the information ontained on the ovals, develop topic sentences and supporting details to form three paragraphs.

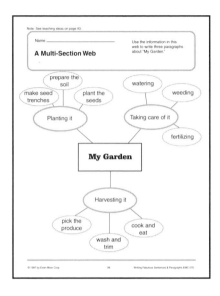

Practice using a multi-section web:

- Make a transparency of the blank web on page 99. Guide students through the following steps to complete the web. Fill in the ovals as they contribute answers.

---

1. Select a subject and write it in the large center rectangle.

2. Think of two or more important things to say about the subject. Write these ideas in the middle-sized ovals. These become the main ideas for each paragraph.

3. Put supporting information for each main idea in the small ovals surrounding it.

- To write from the web, work with one section at a time to create paragraphs. Develop a good topic sentence for the main idea of each paragraph. Then use the supporting details to write the other sentence.

Name _____

A One-Section Web

Develop a topic sentence about puppies.

Write sentences that tell supporting details.

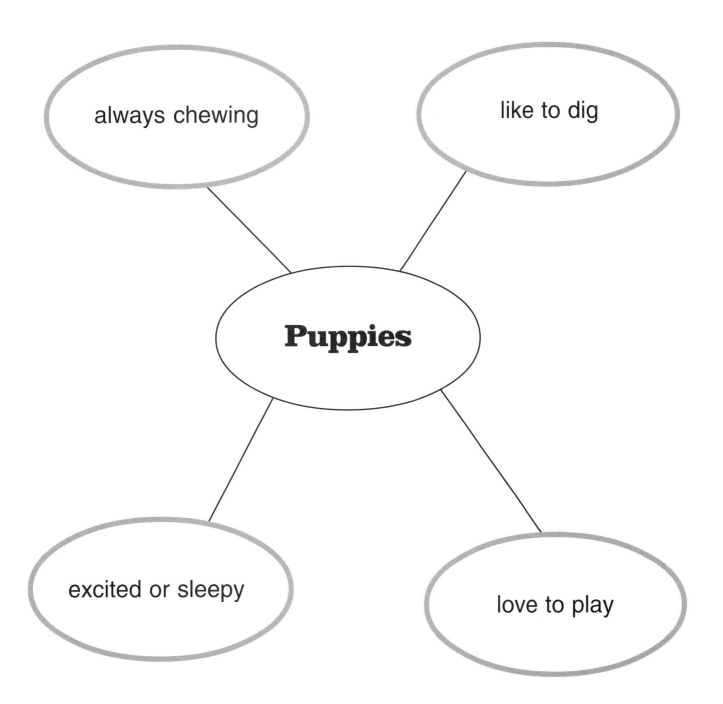

Name _____

Write a Paragraph

Develop a topic sentence about blizzards.

Write sentences that tell supporting details.

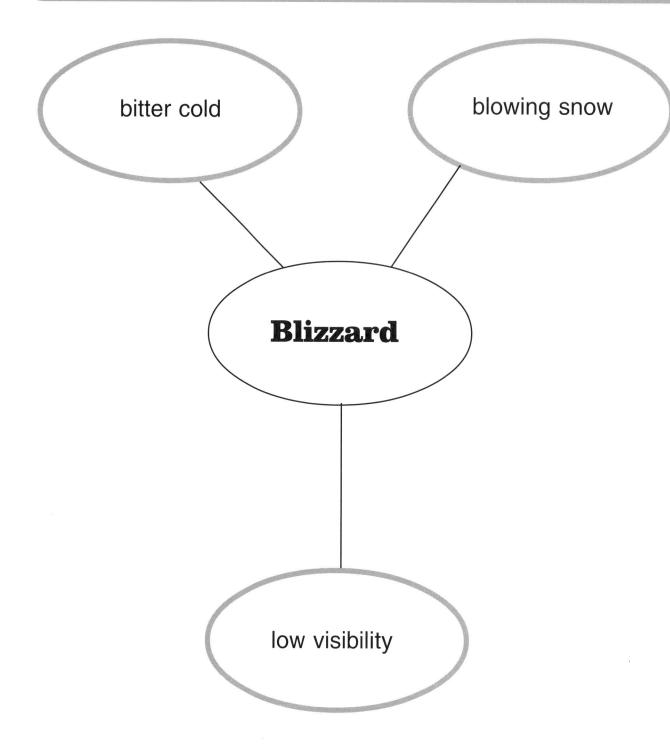

bitter cold

blowing snow

Blizzard

low visibility

Name _____

Add supporting details.
Then write a paragraph.

Complete the Web

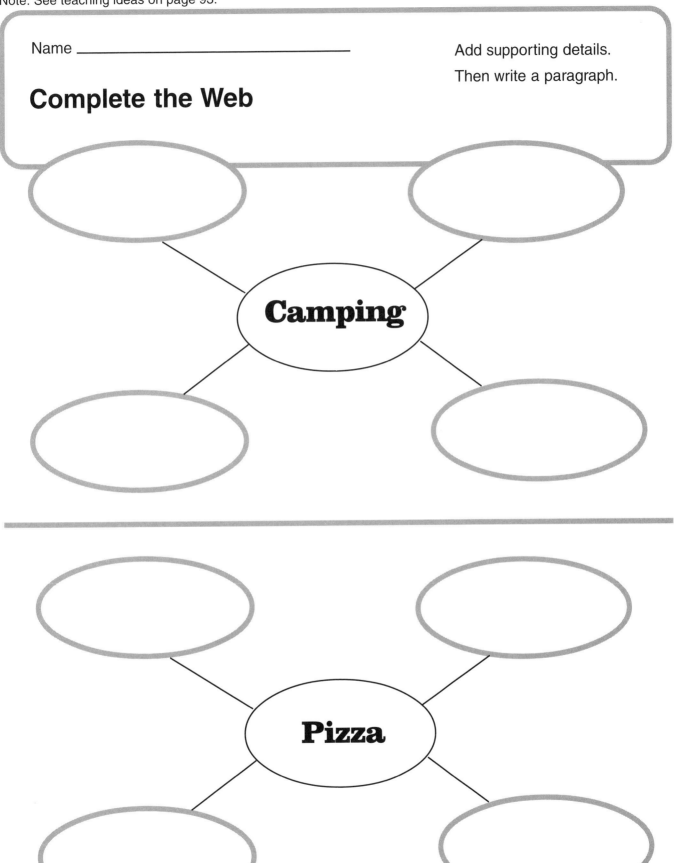

Camping

Pizza

Name _____

Use the information in this web to write three paragraphs about "My Garden."

A Multi-Section Web

prepare the soil

make seed trenches

plant the seeds

Planting it

watering

weeding

Taking care of it

fertilizing

My Garden

Harvesting it

pick the produce

wash and trim

cook and eat

Note: See teaching ideas on page 93.

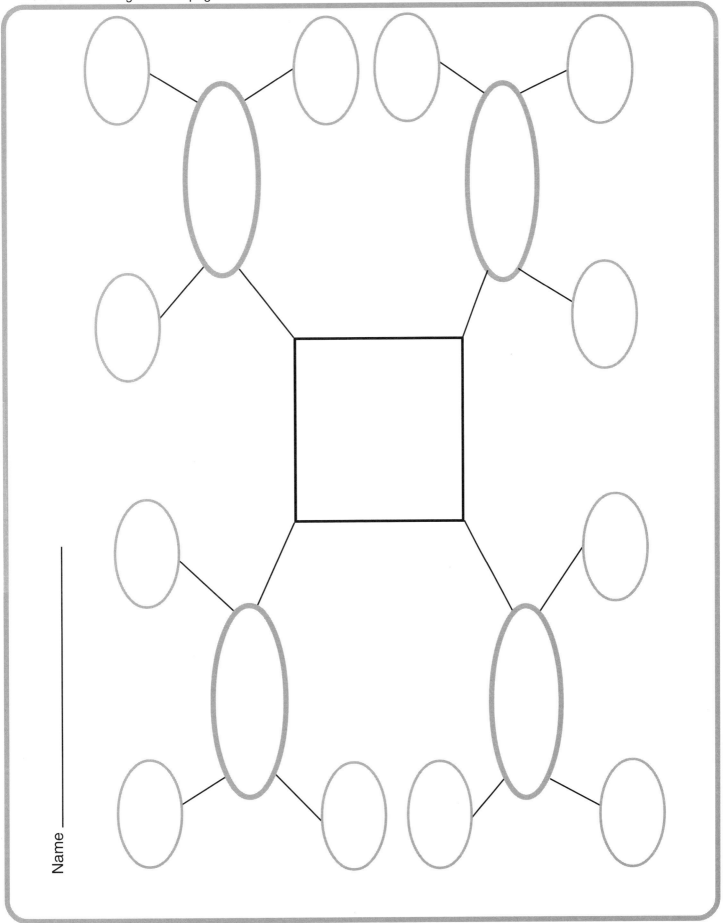

Name _____

Using a Notetaker to Plan Multiple Paragraphs

A notetaker is a helpful tool for organizing information during research activities. It consists of a listing of the general categories of information that the writer intends to include. The notetaker then becomes a plan for paragraphs. It is an outline without the formality.

Introducing Notetakers

Make a transparency of page 101, or enlarge it to create a chart. In introducing the form to your students, explain that each section contains the information that will be included in one paragraph. It will be developed into a topic sentence that gives the main idea and additional sentences which add supporting details. Have students practice writing paragraphs from this completed form.

Additional Notetakers

The notetakers on pages 102-105 provide categories for four different report genres. Practice with one or more of these so that students will be able to use them independently throughout the year to assist with writing assignments in these topic areas.

As the need arises, develop your own notetakers.

Notetakers
Help to Organize Information

Name _____

Notetaker

Name of animal:

Greater Fruit Bat

Range:

South and SE Asia

Writing
About an
Animal

Physical characteristics/ special adaptations:

long muzzle, large eyes,
pointy ears, furry body,
5 ft. wingspan, keen vision
and sense of smell

Habitat:

forests in tropical and
subtropical climates with
year-round supply of fruit

Food:

bananas and other tropical
fruits

Enemies:

man, urbanization

Interesting facts/habits/behaviors:

crushes fruit between
peglike teeth, polinates
night-blooming trees and
plants, spreads seeds

Outlook for future:

habitats being reduced as
tropical forests are cut

Notetaker

Name _____

Writing About a Person

Who
(name)

When
(he/she lives or lived)

Where (he/she lives or lived)

What (he/she does or did)

Why (it is important to know about him/her)

Notetaker

Name _____

Writing About a **Place**

Name of place:

_____

Reason for name:

_____

_____

Geographic location:

_____

_____

_____

_____

People who live there:

_____

_____

_____

_____

Significance to history:

_____

_____

_____

_____

Future significance:

_____

_____

_____

_____

Notetaker

Name _____

Name of animal:

_____

Range:

_____

Writing About an **Animal**

Physical characteristics/ special adaptations:

_____
_____
_____

Habitat:

_____
_____
_____

Food:

_____
_____
_____

Enemies:

_____
_____
_____

Interesting facts/habits/behaviors:

_____
_____
_____

Outlook for future:

_____
_____

Note: See teaching ideas on page 100.

Notetaker

Name _____

Name of event:

When:

Writing
About an
Event

What is it:

_____

_____

_____

Who does it involve:

_____

_____

_____

Significance:

_____

_____

_____

Where did it occur:

_____

_____

_____

Why:

_____

_____

_____

_____

_____

_____

_____

Using An Outline to Plan
Multiple Paragraphs

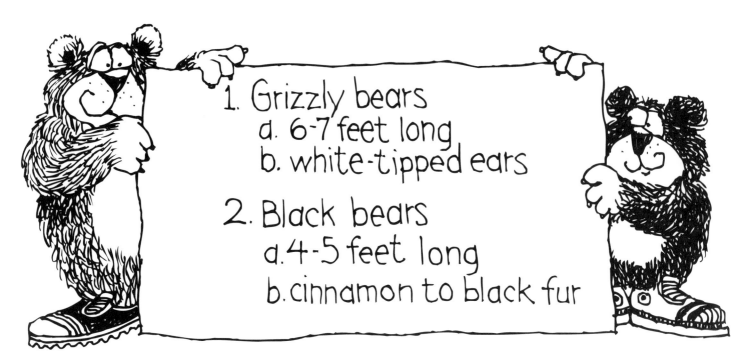

1. Grizzly bears
   a. 6-7 feet long
   b. white-tipped ears

2. Black bears
   a. 4-5 feet long
   b. cinnamon to black fur

Outlining is another organizational method that can be used when students are writing a report or story requiring more than one paragraph.

Page 107 provides an outline form showing an outline of information about a plan for taking care of the earth.

- Make a transparency of page 107, or enlarge it to create a chart.

- Introduce this outline form to your students. Explain that each section will become one paragraph of their report or story. Each paragraph will need a topic sentence that gives the main idea and additional sentences which give supporting details.

Page 108 provides an outline form with main ideas in place. Students should fill in supporting details and then write paragraphs that include the information in the outline.

Page 109 provides a blank outline form to use when students are ready to develop their own outlines.

An Outline Organizes Information

A Plan for Taking Care of the Earth

I. A plan is needed
   A. Limited resources
   B. Increased demands
   C. Future in jeopardy

II. Reduce
   A. Limit paper products
   B. Use native plants when landscaping
   C. Carpool

III. Reuse
   A. Create a treasure drawer
   B. Carryalls from plastic gallon containers
   C. Clothing bank

IV. Recycle
   A. Paper
   B. Aluminum
   C. Glass

Subject of the Report

Main Idea
will become the topic sentence of a paragraph

Supporting Details
will become the additional sentences of the paragraph

Name _____

**An Outline Organizes
Information**

How to Play _____
(name of game)

I. Equipment you need

    A. _____

    B. _____

    C. _____

II. How to play the game

    A. _____

    B. _____

    C. _____

III. How to keep score

    A. _____

    B. _____

    C. _____

Name _____

┌─────────────────────────────────────┐
│ (subject)   │
│   │
│   │
└─────────────────────────────────────┘

I. _____

    A. _____

    B. _____

    C. _____

II. _____

    A. _____

    B. _____

    C. _____

III. _____

    A. _____

    B. _____

    C. _____

Note: Use this checklist with students as they write independent paragraphs on subjects of their own choosing.

Paragraph Writing Checklist

Put a check in the box when you have completed the step.

☐ 1. Pick a subject for your paragraph.

☐ 2. Learn about the subject.

☐ 3. Think about what the main idea of the paragraph will be.

☐ 4. Write a topic sentence about the main idea.

☐ 5. Add details to your paragraph.

   Does each detail support the main idea?

☐ 6. Read your paragraph.

   How can you make it better?

   Does it make sense?

☐ 7. Proofread your paragraph.

   (You may want to ask a friend to proofread it also.)

   Spelling corrected _____

   First word indented _____

   End punctuation for sentences correct _____

   Content accurate _____

☐ 8. Prepare your final copy.

Answer Key

Page 8

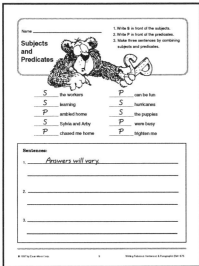

Can You Find the Sentences?

Find the groups of words that are sentences.
Label their parts:
1. Circle the subject of the sentence.
2. Draw a line under the predicate of the sentence.
Write "sentence" on the line following each complete sentence.

Tom and Julie played ball — *Sentence*
Climbed the mountain and camped —
The class went to the library — *Sentence*
Marilyn ate her lunch — *Sentence*
Susan, Bill, and Jack —
The flag waved in the wind — *Sentence*
The girl stumbled forward — *Sentence*
Always busy working in the kitchen, the cooks —
The soccer ball flew into the goal — *Sentence*
The computer responded to his command — *Sentence*

On the back of this page, make each non-sentence into a sentence.

Page 9

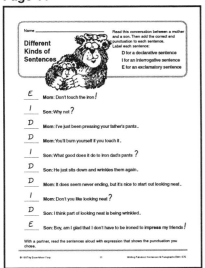

Subjects and Predicates

1. Write S in front of the subjects.
2. Write P in front of the predicates.
3. Make three sentences by combining subjects and predicates.

S the workers
S learning
P ambled home
S Sylvia and Arby
P chased me home
P can be fun
S hurricanes
S the puppies
P were busy
P frighten me

Sentences:
1. *Answers will vary.*
2.
3.

Page 11

Different Kinds of Sentences

Read this conversation between a mother and a son. Then add the correct end punctuation to each sentence.
Label each sentence:
D for a declarative sentence
I for an interrogative sentence
E for an exclamatory sentence

E Mom: Don't touch the iron!
I Son: Why not?
D Mom: I've just been pressing your father's pants.
D Mom: You'll burn yourself if you touch it.
I Son: What good does it do to iron dad's pants?
D Son: He just sits down and wrinkles them again.
D Mom: It does seem never ending, but it's nice to start out looking neat.
I Mom: Don't you like looking neat?
D Son: I think part of looking neat is being wrinkled.
E Son: Boy, am I glad that I don't have to be ironed to impress my friends!

With a partner, read the sentences aloud with expression that shows the punctuation you chose.

Page 13

From the Journal of a Crayon

"Boy, is it crowded in here! That Jungle Green is in my spot. Will you please move? I wish that they would make these boxes bigger!"

"Stop complaining! Soon one of us will be lost or broken and then there'll be plenty of room."

I listened and observed as the hushed conversation in my crayon-box home droned on. It was a new sixty-four color box with a tight lid and bright yellow and green triangles covering its front. Few crayon users realize that crayons not only speak but they also have feelings. Just the other day, I witnessed the dismay of a canary yellow whose tip was nibbled off by a hungry artist, and the sorrow of a twenty-box that had lost its black. Imagine life without a black! Well, it is true that crayons do have the sensitive souls of artists and it is time for all humankind to recognize it. How can we as crayons make our position known?

I have taken it upon myself to represent the crayon world. I will present a case for our humane treatment at the National Rights Conference to be held in Washington, D.C., on June 1. Soon all crayons will enjoy the notoriety of Harold's purple crayon. It will be a red-letter day for all writers of color!

Page 16
1. Carrying their helmets in their hands, the football team ran onto the field.
2. Using the library browser, Pam found a book for her report.
3. As the clown ran around the elephant, the elephant squirted water on the clown.
4. By the way Joe sounded on the telephone, I could tell he didn't feel well. Or... When I called Joe on the telephone, he sounded like he didn't feel well.
5. After last night's snow storm, the fenceposts poked their tops above the drifts.
6. When Tom fell off his bike, he learned that racing bikes can be dangerous.

Page 18
1. John, my little brother, is a good shortstop.
2. Sandy, a frisky puppy, likes to chase the cat.
3. Scott's goldfish, Force of Freedom, survived for five years.
4. My friends, Sandy, Carlos, and Willy, like to play in the park.
5. Mr. Sutter, my coach, taught me how to hit the ball hard.
6. Ashley, my next door neighbor, feeds my puppies when I'm gone.

Page 20
1. Grandma made chocolate chip cookies for me and snickerdoodles for my brother Jim.
2. The horse nibbled the hay while he swished his tail to keep the flies away.
3. My umbrella broke when the wind blew, and I got soaked. Or... I got soaked because my umbrella broke when the wind blew.
4. Mowing the lawn is hard work, so my mom always brings me lemonade when I finish.
5. The mail carrier brought a package because it's my father's birthday today.
6. My glasses steamed up when I went inside because it was freezing outside.

Page 21
1. Autumn, sometimes called fall, is a season of the year. Or... Autumn, a season of the year, is sometimes called fall.
2. When the leaves turn color, squirrels begin to store nuts and seeds for the winter.
3. Spectators don coats and gloves because the air is crisp and cold.
4. The sun is sleeping when I get up and it goes to bed while I eat my dinner.
5. Autumn, a celebration of the harvest, is also a warning to prepare for the cold days ahead.

Page 40
Paragraph One: Main idea — teeth have jobs
Topic Sentence — Teeth have three important jobs.

Page 41
Paragraph One: Main idea — lantern fish give off their own light
Topic Sentence — Lantern fish live near the bottom of the ocean where it is very dark, so they carry their own lights.

Paragraph Two: Main idea — backswimmers swim upside down
Topic Sentence — The backswimmer spends most of its time upside-down.

Paragraph Three: Main idea — Martin Luther King was an influential leader
Topic Sentence — Martin Luther King had a special talent for leadership.

Page 42
Paragraph One: Main idea — centipedes are hunters
Topic Sentence — The centipede is a hunter.

Paragraph Two: Main idea — Charlie McCarthy was a star
Topic Sentence— Even a puppet can be a famous star.

Paragraph Three: Main idea — quicksand is caused by water moving through regular sand
Topic Sentence — So quicksand is not a special kind of sand, it is just the result of water trying to move through plain old sand.

Page 43
Paragraph One: Main idea — making jelly beans takes a week
Topic Sentence — It takes a week to make a jelly bean.

Paragraph Two: Main idea — you can figure out how far away lightning is
Topic Sentence: The lightning is a mile way for every five seconds that you count, so you can "measure" how far the lightning is from you.

Paragraph Three: Main idea — Piñatas are special Mexican party items
Topic Sentence — The piñata, a decorated container filled with candy and small treats, is an important festival tradition.

Page 44
Paragraph One: Main idea — water cycle
Topic Sentence — The same water moves from liquid form to water vapor and back to liquid form over and over again.

Paragraph Two: Main idea — Man's first flight was short
Topic Sentence — The flight lasted only twelve seconds, but that twelve seconds marked the beginning of a new era in transportation - travel by air.

Paragraph Three: Main idea — Jesse Owens started poor, but became a world hero.
Topic Sentence — Jesse Owens, sometimes called the World's Fastest Human, began life as a poor sharecropper's son and became a world hero.

Page 45
Paragraph One: Topic sentence — Sentence 1
Details: Sentences 2, 3, and 4

Paragraph Two: Topic sentence — Sentence 2
Details: Sentences 3, 4, 5, and 6

Page 46
Paragraph One: Topic sentence — Sentence 8
Details: Sentences 1, 4, 5, and 6

Paragraph Two: Topic sentence — Sentence 1
Details: Sentences 2, 3, 4, 5

Page 47
Topic sentence — Sentence 1
Details: sentences 3, 4, 8, and 9.

Page 48
Paragraph One — Hummingbirds can barely walk.

Paragraph Two — He has red hair and blue eyes.

Paragraph Three — Today space shuttles routinely take off and return to the Earth on various space missions.

Page 49
Paragraph One — By radio telephone the distress signal is "Mayday."

Paragraph Two — Halloween is fun too.

Paragraph Three — Cats sleep as much as twenty hours a day.

Page 83 The First Americans

Several million people lived in North America before the arrival of Europeans. The Native Americans called themselves by the names of their tribes. Some of the people were hunters and others were farmers. The hunters moved across the land killing only the animals that they needed for food, tools, clothing, and shelter.

There were hundreds of tribes in America when Christopher Columbus arrived and thought that he was in India. Columbus called all of the tribes "Indians" even though the people that he referred to were scattered all over the country, spoke different languages, and had different customs.

The history of the Native Americans following the Europeans' discover of America if a story of hardship. The Europeans brought many sicknesses with them that the Native Americans had never seen. Some Europeans wanted the Native Americans to change the ways that they lived. Native Americans believed that the land was for everyone to use and share. The Europeans wanted to take over and claim the new land as theirs.

When the United States became an independent nation, the government started moving the Native Americans off their land and giving it to the white settlers. By the late 1800s most Native Americans were forced to live on reservations.

Today there are hundreds of reservations located in thirty-four states. Many Native Americans live on these reservations. They proudly hold onto their tribal customs and teach the history of their people to their children. Other Native Americans live in cities and towns across the United States.

In 1924, the Snyder Act made all Native Americans citizens of the United States. So today Native Americans are members of two groups. As citizens of the United States, they vote, pay taxes, and serve in the military. As citizens of their tribal nations, they take part in their tribal government and can choose to live on or off their tribal lands.